The *Great* Awakening

Foreword by
Richard Harris

Andrew Wommack

Published in partnership between Andrew Wommack Ministries and Harrison House Publishers.

Woodland Park, CO 80863 – Shippensburg, PA 17257

ISBN 13 TP: 978-1-59548-719-3

For Worldwide Distribution, Printed in the USA

1 2 3 4 5 6 / 27 26 25 24

Contents

Foreword

by Richard Harris
Truth & Liberty Executive Director

The Bible says do "*not* [forsake] *the assembling of* [your-selves] *together*" (Heb. 10:25). We have the God-given right to assemble and worship God, and our ministry took a stand against the government's efforts to take these rights away during Covid. Many people feared we could pay a huge price because of this bold stand, but God prospered us. That's not just true for us, it's true for many ministries that stood strong for freedom and truth during that time.

Pastors Jack Hibbs, Che Ahn, and Rob McCoy in California all defied government orders to shut down. They were fined millions of dollars. But in the end, those fines were all struck down as unconstitutional and their churches grew by massive amounts!

I don't deny that things have gotten very bad in our country, but the Third Great Awakening is underway, and we are starting to see evidence of it. In 2023, a revival happened at little Asbury College—a Christian school in Wilmore, Kentucky—that drew 50,000 people from all over the world, mostly Gen-Z young adults.[1]

Revival also seemed to be spreading to a number of other colleges around America,[2] including secular universities like Texas A&M and Auburn.[3] There were so many students getting saved at the University of Georgia, that they were being baptized in the backs of pickup trucks![4] A recent study by the Barna Group shows that church attendance among Millennials actually went up by 18 percent from 2019 to 2022, and Gen Z church attendance is up 8 percent over that same period.[5]

John Sorenson, president of Evangelism Explosion, said on an episode of our Truth & Liberty Show that the organization saw 70 million people come to Christ around the world in 2023.[6]

Over Easter weekend in 2024, more than 1,600 people were baptized at a Florida beach.[7] On Pentecost Sunday of the same year, about 12,000 people were baptized off a California beach, reportedly the largest mass baptism ever in U.S. history.[8]

You may be really surprised to know this, but the legal restrictions that liberals imposed on our freedom of religion in America over the last seventy years are actually falling away. There have been a series of cases from the United States Supreme Court over the last three years that have brought us closer to the Founding Father's "original intent." One of those cases was *Kennedy v. Bremerton School District*.

In that case, Joe Kennedy, a U.S. Marine veteran who was coaching football at Bremerton High School in Washington state felt that he should go to the fifty-yard line of the field after every game to pray. He would kneel and silently thank God and ask His blessings on the players.

After a while, players started to voluntarily join him. He never once told any player they had to pray with him. But the school district fired him anyway. Coach Joe, like all true Marines, stood his ground and fought back. He took his case all the way to the U.S. Supreme Court. The Court found in Joe's favor and, when they did, they overturned another bad ruling—*Lemon v. Kurtzman*.

Joe's lawyer, Kelly Shackelford, leads First Liberty and is a frequent guest on our Truth & Liberty Show. He explained that the "Lemon Test" was the basis for 7,000 lower court cases since 1971 that restricted religious freedom in America. He said that, in doing away with that wrong standard, the Supreme Court has expanded religious freedom in America to a point we have not seen in seventy years![9]

We heard from Coach Joe in person at our 2024 Truth & Liberty Awards Banquet, where we gave him the Samuel Whittemore Award for Courageous Christian Citizenship. It was powerful to hear him humbly talk about why he did what he did—because it was the right thing to do!

As you read this booklet, be encouraged by the good things that are happening in America regarding our religious freedoms, and particularly the words that the Lord has given Andrew about the future. I believe as you read, you'll see that this nation's best years are still ahead, and that together, Christians can make a difference!

Introduction

Are you troubled by what's going on in the world and waiting for God to do something about it? Do you want to get involved and make a difference, but don't know where to start? Is there anything the body of Christ can do to respond? If you believe everything you hear or read in the news, it may seem like America is going in a negative direction, ungodliness has taken over our culture, and the moral fabric of the nation is unraveling at an alarming rate.

There are people out there who think they are motivating Christians to act by only sharing bad news. I'll admit there are things happening in this nation that I thought I'd never see in my lifetime. But there are also good things to report! We've seen some things happen around the nation that prove God is working. The Lord has also shown me some things that have me really encouraged!

God has spoken to me on several occasions over the years about things to come, but it's what He shared with me in 2021 that has really changed my perspective. I believe the body of Christ can make a difference, and we will win if we just don't quit.

Back in 2015, the U.S. Supreme Court's ruling on so-called "gay marriage" really got my attention, and I decided to do something as a result of it. Along with several friends, we formed the Truth & Liberty Coalition to address issues like abortion, homosexuality, socialism, and other things that are contrary to the Word of God. As the body of Christ, we wanted to make a difference in our culture by speaking out about moral issues and dealing with current events.

Since then, we've created the Truth & Liberty Show where we have addressed these and other issues from a biblical perspective. We have hosted numerous events where the movers and shakers in this nation—including Lance Wallnau, David Barton of WallBuilders, William J. "Bill" Federer, and many others—have shared about what Christians can do to make a difference. We've also hosted candidate forums, distributed more than two million voter guides to help believers vote according to biblical values, and created a website that is a clearinghouse for the best resources to help Christians stand for truth.

But it's going to take the body of Christ standing up and turning our nation back toward biblical values. America is a world leader, and as this nation goes, so goes the world. I believe we are in the middle of something only seen a few times in this nation's history. If Christians get involved and take a stand, we will see things change for the better!

The Gift of Prophecy

Now there are diversities of gifts, but the same Spirit. And there are differences of administrations, but the same Lord. And there are diversities of operations, but it is the same God which worketh all in all. But the manifestation of the Spirit is given to every man to profit withal.

1 Corinthians 12:4–7

Before we go much further, it is important to understand what the Bible means by the gift of prophecy and how it is different from the ministry of a prophet. Maybe you didn't know this, but God has anointed me to be a prophet. I'm not saying this for any purpose except to establish that I will at times receive a word from the Lord and share it with the body of Christ.

Now, failure to understand the difference between the simple gift of prophecy (1 Cor. 12:10) available to all believers and the ministry of a prophet (Eph. 4:11) has led to some strange things being called words of prophecy in many churches.

Some people actually prepare teachings during the week and deliver them as prophecies in church. Others use "prophecy" as an opportunity to rebuke someone, vent their prejudices, or put in their "two bits" about what the church should be doing. None of those things are the gift of prophecy that the Apostle Paul was describing in 1 Corinthians 12.

The fourth verse reveals that the spiritual gifts are all of the Holy Spirit. The fifth verse reveals that the way they are administered is subject to Jesus. The sixth verse shows that God the Father is the one working all of these gifts through all the different ways. In other words, Paul was saying that God is the one working all these gifts in all people. The Father, Son, and Holy Spirit are directly in control of all the gifts of the Spirit, so people are not free to do "their own thing" with these gifts.

According to 1 Corinthians 14:3, the simple gift of prophecy that operates in the church assembly is limited to general edification, exhortation, and comfort of the church body. Therefore, what Paul was describing in 1 Corinthians 12 will never be a lengthy teaching, a rebuke, or a warning. It will just be words of encouragement from the Lord along the lines of "Children, I love you," "I've received your praise," or "I'm present to minister to you."

If a person gives an individual prophecy of personal direction to someone, that is the ministry of a prophet and is different from the simple gift of prophecy.

Believers wouldn't allow people called to the office of a teacher to interrupt a service and just start teaching. That would be out of order. Teachers should make themselves known to the pastor, and if given the authority, then they could teach. Likewise, people who minister direction or future events to an individual or the whole body and claim that it is a prophecy are out of order. That would be the ministry of a prophet, and prophets should be recognized by the pastor, just as teachers would have to be.

The Ministry of the Prophet

And he gave some, apostles; and some, prophets; and some, evangelists; and some, pastors and teachers;

*for the perfecting of the saints, for the work of the
ministry, for the edifying of the body of Christ.*

Ephesians 4:11–12

The ministry gift of a prophet is one of the five-fold
ministry gifts to the church and is different from the simple
gift of prophecy. In 2014, Kenneth Copeland laid hands on
me at a ministers' conference and imparted the ministry of
a prophet to me. He said,

> *Up to now, you have ministered in the office of the
> teacher. But tonight, by the command of the Lord
> Jesus Christ, head of the church, I separate you to
> the office of the prophet, in Jesus' name. And every
> spiritual gift—every endowment from on high nec-
> essary to carry out this assignment—is imparted to
> you now, from heaven through the earth to you.*[10]

What he shared in front of all these ministers confirmed some things that the Lord had already shown me
and that I had been meditating on for some time.

Now, I still function primarily as a teacher, but there are
things that God shares with me that I share with the body
of Christ. So, I do believe that God speaks prophetically

through me. In one instance, the Lord spoke to me in 2021 and dramatically changed my perspective on things happening in this world. It was a deal changer. And since He spoke those things to me, I shared them with the friends and partners of this ministry.

I was in Oklahoma City at a meeting called The Encounter. My niece and nephew hosted the event along with some other Charis Bible College graduates. I was so pleased to see them hosting this event where there were about 700 people. My niece and nephew were just starting in ministry and were already way ahead of where I started 50 years before. I was so excited to see people coming, the things that were happening, and the maturity they were operating in.

On Friday, March 5, we were worshiping, and the power of the Lord was present. We were singing a song about how the goodness of God "keeps running after me." I was praising God and thanking Him for the encouragement of seeing the younger generation come along, take up the banner, and continue preaching the Gospel.

Then the Lord spoke to me and said, "There are some people in this auditorium who, in the future, will be telling the young people of their generation about what it was like to live during the Third Great Awakening in America."

God Will Heal the Land

If my people, which are called by my name, shall humble themselves, and pray, and seek my face, and turn from their wicked ways; then will I hear from heaven, and will forgive their sin, and will heal their land.

2 Chronicles 7:14

Now, "Great Awakening" is a term I normally wouldn't use! I might have used the terms "revival," "move of God," "a new wave," or something like that. To me, the term "Great Awakening" goes back to the early years of America. The First Great Awakening was back in the 1700s and is what occasioned this nation coming into being.[11] The Second Great Awakening was in the 1800s and led to the end of slavery.[12]

It was clear to me that this wasn't my own thought— this was God speaking to me that we were going to have a Great Awakening. So, I said, "God, are You saying that we are actually going to see a Third Great Awakening?"

I can't tell you how many times I have prayed 2 Chronicles 7:14 over the years. But here's the problem I had: it says "*if my people*" not "*if my person.*" This isn't something that just one person can do. It's talking about the body of Christ—and that they have to "*humble themselves, and pray, and seek [His] face.*" As a nation, had we met the conditions of the Lord's promise? Only God knew.

God has promised that He would heal our land—He would forgive our sins—but we had to do some things first. So, when the Lord said there were people in that room who would be telling the young people of their generation what it was like to be a part of the Third Great Awakening, that excited me.

I said, "God, are You saying that we are actually going to see a Third Great Awakening? Have those conditions been met? Is it going to happen?" When I said that, very clearly the Lord responded to me and said, "No. It's not coming. It's already begun."

I just can't tell you what that did for me. I've been fighting my whole life to see people changed, believing that if enough people were changed, it would change nations. I believe I received a word from the Lord that it's already happening!

Get Confirmation

In the mouth of two or three witnesses shall every word be established.

2 Corinthians 13:1b

Not long after I received this word from the Lord about a Third Great Awakening, I shared it with the partners of our ministry. This was after taking some time to really meditate on the things God had shown me.

Eventually, I spoke about it with my friend, Pastor Duane Sheriff.

Now, there aren't many people in the world who teach the revelation of God's goodness and grace the way I received it from the Lord, but Pastor Duane and I agree on just about every point. We've become good friends and have ministered together a lot over the years.

At the time, Pastor Duane was writing a book called *Counterculture: Answering a Woke Culture with Love, Light, and Life.* In it, he wrote about how there would be a coming Third Great Awakening in America, and the Lord said to him, "That's wrong!" Pastor Duane just stopped right there and asked, "God, isn't there going to be a Third Great Awakening?"

Pastor Duane told me the Lord spoke to him very clearly and said, "No, it's not coming. It's already here!" Wouldn't you know, the next morning he received the email message I sent to our partners about what God had spoken to me in Oklahoma City. When he told me about that, I thought it was really significant. It confirmed what the Lord had shown me.

That reminds me of how we came to the ministry's property in Woodland Park. It's a long story, but back before we built our Bible college campus in Woodland Park, I kept driving past a particular piece of property on the way to our offices in Colorado Springs. I didn't know it at the time, but the man who once owned that property went through a radical conversion just days before his death in the early 1990s and dedicated it to Christian education.

After we purchased the property in 2009, I had the opportunity to speak with the former landowner's family. I found out that he had dedicated the property to God at about the same time the Lord started speaking to me about starting a Bible college.

They told me that the Lord had shown this man a vision of a building with windows looking out on Pike's Peak so students could view the glory of God's creation. I already had plans drawn up for our facilities, including windows that looked out on Pike's Peak. That's awesome!

Awake to Righteousness

Awake to righteousness, and sin not; for some have not the knowledge of God: I speak this to your shame.

1 Corinthians 15:34

In order to truly understand what the Lord is doing in this Third Great Awakening, we should look at what happened during other Great Awakenings in history. After I received that word from the Lord in March 2021, I spoke with David and Tim Barton of WallBuilders, who helped me put some things into perspective. We discussed the history of revival, what to expect during an awakening, and the First and Second Great Awakenings in America.

According to the Bartons, an awakening is different from a revival or a move of God for several reasons. First, the people participating in an awakening typically don't realize it. They may see that they are in a revival, but it's historians looking back who determine whether something was an awakening. Also, an awakening may last decades and not just a few years—it affects people across generations.

While a revival may affect a church or a community in a spiritual way, an awakening has a much broader reach by impacting a region or nation. In other words, it doesn't just stay within the four walls of a church. As it changes lives, people outside the body of Christ take notice.

Also, an awakening doesn't just mean people engage in more prayer or worship. Laws and policies begin to change because of the teaching of the Word of God. Another thing that signifies an awakening is a change in society and culture. People aren't just moved emotionally during an awakening. Discipleship from the Word of God changes people's hearts and minds, and they begin to act and live differently—their behaviors change. Then these same people look at the world around them, at all the injustice, suffering, and sin, and decide to take action! This is why the First Great Awakening brought about America's Declaration of Independence, and the Second Great Awakening brought about the abolition of slavery.

Now, I was around during the charismatic movement of the 1960s, '70s, and '80s. We saw people's lives changed on an individual level, but it didn't qualify as an awakening because society did not change. We're still dealing with a lot of the same social problems today, like abortion, homosexuality, and drug abuse, that really took hold during that time.

For example, I recently watched a popular movie about the Jesus movement in California in the late 1960s and early '70s. I remember hearing about it, but I was in Vietnam for part of that time, so I didn't really get to experience it. It was awesome to see what God was doing and how people's lives were changing individually. But if you go to California today, it is one of the most liberal states in America (as of this writing). So, even though there was a revival that had a spiritual impact on the church, it didn't spread to society as a whole; and the laws and policies didn't reflect that people were turning from ungodliness to righteousness.

Righteousness Exalts a Nation

Righteousness exalteth a nation: but sin is *a reproach to any people.*

Proverbs 14:34

A nation that is not walking in righteousness is walking in disgrace. We should put conforming to God's standards way ahead of considering anybody else's standards. Righteousness is good for everyone, not just the person who executes it. But wickedness oppresses everyone, including the person who is committing it. Therefore, putting righteous people in authority is always preferred.

Our society has devalued godly living and exalted many other things like charisma, looks, money, and connections. But the number one scriptural qualification for leadership is righteousness, which is right standing with God.

> *Moreover thou shalt provide out of all the people able men, such as fear God, men of truth, hating covetousness; and place such over them, to be rulers of thousands, and rulers of hundreds, rulers of fifties, and rulers of tens.*

Exodus 18:21

In this verse, Jethro was instructing Moses to choose men who could help him govern the Israelites after they left Egypt. Notice the qualifications for these men: they should fear God, be men of truth, and hate covetousness.

These men wouldn't be appointed to lead based on skills or talents. It was all about integrity. You can teach skills, but you can't teach integrity. That's something that has to come from the heart.

This system placed a leader over every ten people in the nation. The first step to resolve a dispute would be to go to the person who was over ten people, and then take the matter up the chain of command until it was resolved. If this system sounds familiar, it's because this is one of the verses our Founding Fathers used to draft the U.S. Constitution and establish the government of this nation as a constitutional republic (not a democracy).[13] See, despite what some people would have you believe, America is a Christian nation, and it was founded on biblical principles.

For example, the three branches of the federal government—judicial, legislative, and executive—were based on Isaiah 33:22.[14]

> *For the Lord is our judge, the Lord is our lawgiver,*
> *the Lord is our king; he will save us.*

There are examples like this all throughout America's founding documents because the majority of our Founding Fathers were influenced by the Bible, and many of them were Christians.[15] They ensured that people would be able to worship freely by placing that God-given right in the First Amendment of the Bill of Rights. Yet, there are people today who want to promote ungodliness and keep God out of the public square.

"Separation of Church and State"

The woman shall not wear that which pertaineth unto a man, neither shall a man put on a woman's garment: for all that do so are abomination unto the Lord thy God.

Deuteronomy 22:5

Back in 2021, I heard about a member of Congress who quoted from the Bible during a debate in the U.S. House of Representatives. The legislation being considered—something called the "Equality Act"—would have imposed pro-homosexuality, pro-transgender, and pro-abortion policies on Christian organizations. This representative read from Deuteronomy 22:5, which says, "*The woman shall not wear that which pertaineth unto a man, neither shall a man put on a woman's garment: for all that do so* are *abomination unto the LORD thy God*." They were arguing that it was wrong for people to act in a way that was contrary to biology—that the transgender movement was an offense against God.

This member of Congress said the bill would go directly against what is laid out in Scripture. I realize that may be a strong statement for some people, but this person was standing on God's Word to make their point. But some people don't let the Bible get in the way of what they believe, and that's why we've seen all these ungodly things in this nation.

Well, it caused no small stir! A number of other representatives criticized this person for quoting the Bible, and one went as far to say, "What any religious tradition describes as God's will is no concern of this Congress."[16]

That's just terrible! That is so contrary to what our Founding Fathers believed and what this nation was founded upon. You may have heard people talk about how "separation of church and state" is an idea found in the Constitution, and that's why there shouldn't be prayer in schools, why the Ten Commandments shouldn't be displayed in public, or why the Bible shouldn't be quoted in Congress.

Well, that phrase isn't actually in the Constitution. It was taken from a letter written by one of the Founders, President Thomas Jefferson, to a group of Baptist pastors. In it, he was talking about how the government shouldn't be involved in church business or restrict their freedom of religion.[17] It doesn't say anything about Christians not participating in government or banning God and his Word from our government.

As a matter of fact, the U.S. Capitol building, where our Congress meets in Washington, DC, was once used as a church building, with the approval of both the House of Representatives and the Senate! Just two days after he wrote that letter to the Baptist pastors, Jefferson attended church in the Capitol and listened to a sermon by his good friend, Rev. John Leland.[18] That's awesome!

You see, some historians claim that not every Founding Father was a Christian, and that may be true to some extent. But they can't say that they weren't influenced by the Bible, didn't attend church, and didn't support the spread of Christianity in this nation.

Signs of an Awakening

The First and Second Great Awakenings brought about fundamental changes in society and culture, and I believe we are already seeing evidence that the Third Great Awakening is underway here in America. Some people—even in the body of Christ—may not acknowledge it, but I can see positive signs.

One of the most encouraging things that happened in our nation was on June 24, 2022, when the United States Supreme Court issued a 6–3 majority decision in the *Dobbs v. Jackson Women's Health Organization* case. It overturned the *Roe v. Wade* ruling that resulted in the deaths of more than 63 million children since 1973.

The Court sided with the original meaning of the U.S. Constitution—sending the issue of the right to life back to the states to decide. We should express our gratitude to the Lord for the brave men and women who defended the Constitution and made this decision, along with all the people who stood on the Word of God as they worked against abortion all these years!

Over the years, around the anniversary of the *Roe v Wade* decision, I have hosted many pro-life activists on my *Gospel Truth* television program. People like Kristan Hawkins of Students for Life of America, Melissa Ohden of Abortion Survivors Network, Marjorie Dannenfelser of SBA Pro-Life America, and others fought tooth and toenail to get this ruling off the books.

Our friend Janet Folger Porter has been leading the way in this fight for years. I'll tell you, she is stronger than horseradish! If it weren't for her work in drafting "heartbeat bills" around the country, many states wouldn't have been ready for the end of *Roe*. She has taken a stand for life and has had a huge impact!

Today, in twenty-three states, abortion is now illegal after conception or the baby's heartbeat can be detected, and it's illegal at later stages of pregnancy in seven other states.[19] Thousands of babies' lives are being saved every year because of the overturn of *Roe v. Wade*.[20]

I'm grateful to God for each one of these ladies. They had confidence that what they were doing was going to make a difference. Because of what the Lord did through them—because they were willing and obedient—on the day of the *Dobbs* ruling, many states already had laws in place to protect life and close the doors of abortion clinics forever!

At the 2023 Truth & Liberty Conference, we presented a dramatic stage production called *Overturned*, which tells the story of the rise and fall of the abortion movement in America. It shows how abortion not only takes the innocent lives of millions of babies every year, but it also negatively affects the lives of everyone involved. The most impactful part of the production was how people who've experienced an abortion can find redemption in Jesus. It's powerful!

We need to celebrate what God has done, working through Bible-believing people who stand for the sanctity of life and inspiring the constitutionally conservative justices of the Supreme Court to make a decision that will save countless lives! It's encouraging to see things turning around in America, that a Great Awakening is underway, and that truth is winning! Praise the Lord!

Stand for Truth

Not long after we received the good report of the *Dobbs* decision, I also heard that one of the conservative justices said the Court should reconsider some other cases—including the one that allowed so-called "gay marriage" (*Obergefell v. Hodges*).[21]

The Word of God has a lot to say about the issues we're facing in society today. If we stay silent, the unbelievers—those who don't have a biblical worldview—will continue being the ones establishing all the policies, determining what we can and can't say, and what we can and can't do.

Now, I've had people challenge me and say, "The Bible doesn't even mention homosexuality. That word's not even in the Bible!" The word "homosexual" wasn't used until the 1800s,[22] so I will admit that the terms "homosexual" and "homosexuality" are not in the Bible. However, the Bible prohibits sexual relations between people of the same sex in several passages. For example, in Leviticus 20:13, the Word says, "*If a man also lie with mankind, as he lieth with a woman, both of them have committed an abomination: they shall surely be put to death; their blood shall be upon them.*" What happened to Sodom and Gomorrah (Gen. 19:1–25) is a pretty good indication of what God thinks of homosexuality.

You will have people come out and call you a bigot, a homophobe, a hate monger, or something else, just because you say things like, "The Bible says that marriage is between a man and a woman." But that doesn't matter. You've got to keep standing on God's Word.

There is a battle going on in America today, but it is not political. Sure, courtrooms and the halls of Congress are battlegrounds, but the war itself is between light and dark—the truth of the Gospel and the lies of the devil. It's between the people of God and the children of the devil.

In this war, the enemy tries to hide behind the mask of political correctness and inclusion. But the real goal is the elimination of God and His influence from society so people can indulge their carnal lifestyles without conviction or guilt.

The way to win this war and save the character of this nation is to change the moral character of its people with the Gospel. I've heard our friend Bill Federer say the most important thing for Christians to do is share the Gospel and get people born again, and the next most important thing is to protect our freedom to keep sharing the Gospel and getting people born again.[23]

It's politically correct to say that homosexuality is genetic—that people are born that way, and we just have to accept it. That is just wrong, wrong, wrong. We need to share the Gospel and help people get born again, then let the Word of God change their way of thinking (Rom. 12:2).

They'll learn that in the beginning, God created them Adam and Eve—man and woman (Gen. 1:27 and Matt. 19:4). But thanks to godly people standing for the truth, we're starting to see things turning around.

Woke Will Go Broke

And this is the condemnation, that light is come into the world, and men loved darkness rather than light, because their deeds were evil. For every one that doeth evil hateth the light, neither cometh to the light, lest his deeds should be reproved.

John 3:19–20

During our 2023 Summer Family Bible Conference at Charis Bible College, the Lord spoke something really encouraging to me.

We typically host our conference during the week of Independence Day, so we had ministry scheduled for the morning of the Fourth of July, along with our patriotic musical production *In God We Trust* later that evening.

Now, I'm unapologetically patriotic, and I love America. As we were just praising and worshiping God, I was thinking about how it was 247 years since the founding of this nation. As I was thanking God for America, the word of the Lord came to me.[24]

In that moment, the Lord told me that in three years, on the 250th anniversary of America's independence, this whole woke movement that has been destroying our nation will be exposed. Things will turn around. Even the mainstream news media—what David Barton calls the "Ten Spies Network"—will have to admit how wrong all these things were.

I believe we are already starting to see evidence of this. We've seen people stand up to companies that are promoting ungodliness, and they are losing huge amounts of money as people boycott their products.[25] Disney, Target, Bud Light, and now, Planet Fitness, have lost hundreds of billions of dollars in sales or stock value after people saw their radical LGBTQ+ policies.[26] Fewer corporations are taking part in Pride Month, which promotes homosexuality and the LGBTQ+ agenda.[27] Many universities are rejecting Diversity, Equity, and Inclusion (DEI) mandates.[28] I recently read that several major corporations have ended their DEI programs.[29]

Even people who practice homosexuality are starting to see that things are going to the extreme, and they are speaking up about things like pornographic books that target children, drag queen shows in libraries, and naked men in gay pride parades. People who aren't even living in a biblically moral way know when things aren't right. But they aren't going to stand for godly lifestyles. That responsibility lies with born-again Christians.

You see, Jesus was the light of the world while He was in it (John 1:4–9), and now we are the light of the world as He shines through us (Matt. 5:14–15). Sinners run from God the way cockroaches run from light. This is why the ungodly fight so hard against morality. They don't want God's light to reveal their deeds for what they are. It's not a liberal versus conservative issue. It's a light versus darkness struggle.

So why isn't the body of Christ as a whole standing up against this wokeness, voting for godly candidates, and otherwise making a bigger impact?

Don't Deny the Creator

For the invisible things of him from the creation of the world are clearly seen, being understood by the things that are made, even *his eternal power and Godhead; so that they are without excuse.*

Romans 1:20

In Romans 1:18–20, the Apostle Paul declared that God revealed Himself to all mankind. Old Testament scriptures proclaim that God revealed Himself through nature (Ps. 19:1–3). We see God in creation because He made the heavens and the earth, and everything in them (Gen. 1:1 and Col. 1:16). But Paul warns that one of the stops on the road to walking away from God is to worship creation rather than the Creator (Rom. 1:25).

According to David Barton, there was a significant split in the American church over the issue of creation in the late 1800s. Just before the American Civil War, Charles Darwin published his book, *The Origin of Species*. In it, Darwin argued that animals and people evolved over millions of years from simple organisms to what we see today. This contradicted the clear teaching of the Bible that God created the earth and everything in it, as recorded in Genesis 1.

Because Darwin's book became so popular, some pastors and Christians began to question the creation story. There are a lot of reasons for that, but it ended up causing many churches to move away from speaking on social and cultural issues. The reasoning was, if the Bible was supposedly wrong about creation, then it could be wrong about other things. These churches decided to focus almost exclusively on getting people saved through evangelizing. This was the birth of what we now call evangelical churches.

Many Christians sided with "science" rather than the Word of God—they started looking at creation rather than the Creator. They embraced Darwinism, withdrew from culture, and focused only on spiritual things, causing ungodliness to take hold in this nation. Teaching evolution eventually became the standard in public schools, which is why so many modern Christians still embrace it, even though the Bible teaches otherwise.

By contrast, there were many churches and pastors who still believed the Bible was the authority on every issue of life. These churches continued preaching the Gospel and teaching on the fundamentals—like marriage, the sanctity of life, and other things—according to God's Word. These people became known as fundamentalists.

According to Dr. Grady McMurtry—a Christian apologist whose work focuses on biblical creation—evolution "justifies the homosexual lifestyle, abortion, euthanasia, racism, pornography, all of our social ills. . . These social issues are merely the branches. The tree trunk is secular humanism, and evolution is the tap root."[30]

Observe All Things

Go ye therefore, and teach all nations, baptizing them in the name of the Father, and of the Son, and of the Holy Ghost: teaching them to observe all things whatsoever I have commanded you: and, lo, I am with you alway, even unto the end of the world. Amen.

Matthew 28:19–20

Jesus called us to "*teach all nations . . . teaching them to observe all things whatsoever I have commanded you.*" Many modern translations of these verses say, "Go and make disciples." The Lord commanded us to go into the world and make disciples. But much of the church has been focused on evangelizing and making converts instead of teaching the fundamentals of the Word of God and making disciples.

Nowadays, we are seeing a growing number of churches—including evangelical churches—embracing the woke movement. They are affirming people who choose to live a homosexual lifestyle, promoting transgenderism, supporting abortion, and all sorts of ungodly things. They may use the Bible to get a person converted, but they are not discipling people about what God has to say about how to live.

Several years ago, I had a Charis student tell me that the school radically changed her life. She said she was an extreme liberal on social issues when she first came, but by graduation, she had become so conservative that many in her own family had nearly disowned her because of her beliefs.

I asked this woman to explain how she had been able to say she loved the Lord, and yet also had been for abortion, homosexuality, transgenderism, and all sorts of other ungodly things. She said, "I loved God, but I didn't love the Bible. When I came to Charis, I learned to love the Word of God, and that changed everything. You can't love God's Word and be a liberal."

David Barton said there has been a dramatic decline in the number of people who are regular readers of the Bible.[31] The youth of this nation used to learn God's Word in our schools. The *New England Primer*, which was a textbook used for over a century, was full of God's Word.[32] Even those who didn't embrace all the truths presented in it were aware of what God's Word said, and it had a restraining influence.

But because many people have forsaken the biblical standard of truth, people today can't even figure out which bathroom to use! I once heard that over ninety percent of pastors believed the Word of God had standards for every area of life but less than ten percent of those same pastors preached on those issues.[33]

Fearfully and Wonderfully Made

I will praise thee; for I am fearfully and wonderfully made: marvellous are thy works; and that my soul knoweth right well. My substance was not hid from thee, when I was made in secret, and curiously wrought in the lowest parts of the earth.

Psalm 139:14–15

The reason evolution is so popular today is because people don't want to accept the fact that they were created by God with a purpose in mind. If they admit to a creator, then they are accountable for their lives. God has a calling for every single person, and all their days were written in a book (Ps. 139:16), which will be opened at judgment (Rev. 20:12). Their works, related to their calling, will be tested by God with fire (1 Cor. 3:13).

But if people can convince themselves that they weren't created but just evolved, then they view themselves as no different than the animals. It leaves them free to fulfill the lusts of the flesh and soothe their consciences while doing it. This is why someone can be convinced that a baby in the womb is just a clump of cells with no life in it.

Ministers have the opportunity to be leaders in their churches and communities. They have a position of influence, but they're not using it. There was a time when the pastor of a church was the most knowledgeable person in town. They would study everything—including economics, politics, health, and science—and be ready to give an answer from the Bible concerning those things. Sad to say, that's lacking in many churches today.

The Bible says that when Elisabeth heard the salutation of Mary, who was pregnant with Jesus, *"the babe leaped in her womb"* (Luke 1:41), referring to John the Baptist; it didn't say "the fetus" or "a clump of cells." Notice also that this baby in the womb was filled with the Holy Spirit. Unfortunately, evolution is all a person ever hears in school and the media, but a pastor who doesn't teach what the Word of God says about life isn't going to counter it.

> *Then the word of the LORD came unto me, saying, Before I formed thee in the belly I knew thee; and before thou camest forth out of the womb I sanctified thee,* and *I ordained thee a prophet unto the nations.*
>
> Jeremiah 1:4–5

Before the prophet Jeremiah was ever born, God was creating him for a purpose. In Galatians 1:15, the Apostle Paul said that God separated him unto the Gospel from his mother's womb. These scriptures are not just for Jeremiah and Paul; they are for everyone. God called us, appointed us, and anointed us while we were in our mother's womb.

Once you realize you were created by God and that you weren't just an accident, you'll want to know why you were created. First and foremost, you were created for relationship with God. That is not limited to, but certainly includes, the born-again experience, where you accept Jesus as your personal Savior. But after salvation, you need to be discipled to fulfill the calling on your life.

Make Disciples

And the things that thou hast heard of me among many witnesses, the same commit thou to faithful men, who shall be able to teach others also.

2 Timothy 2:2

We all have only a limited time here on this earth, so if we aren't doing what this verse says, we and our message will ultimately fail. This has to be our priority. That's why Charis Bible College exists—to disciple and equip people for what God's called them to do so they can go out and change the world for Jesus.

For years, it seemed like I was the one doing all the ministry at our meetings, and I just couldn't minister to all the people who needed it. Maybe you've never thought of this, but there are people you can reach with the Gospel who will never hear from me. That's why we're raising up people to carry this message of God's unconditional love and grace—taking the Gospel farther and deeper than ever before through Charis.

Many of the people who come to our Bible college have their lives radically transformed by just sitting under the Word of God four hours a day, five days a week; they become real disciples. They in turn make other disciples and the kingdom of God continues from generation to generation.

At Charis, we emphasize the truth of God's Word and how it can change a person's life through discipleship. I remember one student who came to school high on meth the first day of class. He had spent years in and out of prison, addicted to drugs, but when he came to Charis, the Lord began to change his life. He took those things to heart, and it made a huge difference.

I remember how this person would shout and praise God in class. I believe God truly transformed his heart more than just his outward expressions of faith. His classmates even nominated him to speak at our Bible college graduation, and he received a standing ovation when he spoke! He is a blessing and truly a trophy of God's grace.

This person ended up going through our Third-Year Practical Government School, and now he serves another organization that encourages pastors and churches to get involved and make an impact in their communities. He has also spoken at some of our events and encouraged Christians to take a stand against the woke ideology that is trying to destroy our nation. It's awesome!

I've watched him grow into a living example of the good things God is doing through this ministry and Bible college. We need a miracle in this nation to turn things around, and I believe what we're doing to raise up disciples is part of the answer. To see someone come from a life of drug abuse now helping churches get involved in their communities is nothing short of miraculous.

Be Salt and Light

Ye are the salt of the earth: but if the salt have lost his savour, wherewith shall it be salted? it is thenceforth good for nothing, but to be cast out, and to be trodden under foot of men. Ye are the light of the world. A city that is set on an hill cannot be hid.

Matthew 5:13–14

Several years ago, we had a former U.S. senator and presidential candidate speak at our Charis Bible College. After he left office, he redirected his attention to getting Christians involved in turning the nation back toward godly values. He told us how Christians have to quit hiding in their churches, get out in the marketplace, and change the culture.

This man shared a lot of his views on what was happening in America, and I was really encouraged. He said that after campaigning for president, he was more optimistic than ever about the future of our nation. I was kind of surprised about that because his views had been mercilessly attacked in the media.

Despite those things, he became convinced the majority of Americans are not for all the ungodliness that is going on. But he assessed that the ungodly are more committed to changing this nation than the godly are to preserving it. I tend to agree with him. You see, we are the salt of the earth. To do any good, we have to "get out of the saltshaker" and start being salt and light to the world.

The blame for the way our nation is heading today lies at the feet of the church, and more specifically, ministers. Charles G. Finney was one of the most prominent preachers of the Second Great Awakening. He famously said in a message to pastors:

> *If immorality prevails in the land, the fault is ours in a great degree. If there is a decay of conscience, the pulpit is responsible for it. If the public press lacks moral discrimination, the pulpit is responsible for it. If the church is degenerate and worldly, the pulpit is responsible for it. If the world loses its interest in religion, the pulpit is responsible for it. If Satan rules in our halls of legislation, the pulpit is responsible for it. If our politics become so corrupt that the very foundations of our government are ready to fall away, the pulpit is responsible for it.*[34]

Finney was saying that pastors and the church have a responsibility to the nation to promote morality. But the vast majority of Christians aren't being taught about what the Bible has to say about the issues, and pastors just aren't taking a stand for truth.

Teach from the Word

Then said Jesus to those Jews which believed on him, If ye continue in my word, then *are ye my disciples*

43

indeed; and ye shall know the truth, and the truth shall make you free.

John 8:31–32

I once visited with a minister who, from the pulpit, was intentionally silent on the issue of homosexuality. He said, "I want to love these people. I don't want to condemn anybody or turn them away."

I agree that we aren't supposed to condemn people and we should love them, but I asked him, "What about the kids who are growing up in your church?" I told this pastor that the secular world is very aggressive in promoting its agenda. If the church doesn't stand up and say what is right and preach the Word, then the views of the world will be forced on young people. They'll believe lies and adopt views that are contrary to the Word of God. "It's wonderful to make people feel welcome to come to your church," I said. "But you're not doing them any favors by not speaking the truth."

This pastor said, "I never thought of that."

The church at large has basically retreated to just preaching about the born-again experience—whether people are going to heaven or not. While this is happening, the world is preaching their doctrine. Sadly, a lot of Christians are buying into this because there isn't an opposing voice or anyone standing up for the truth.

I can think of a number of people, including our friend Janet Boynes, who left homosexuality because Christians were loving enough to share the truth of God's Word. Now, Janet has her own ministry where she helps other people overcome same-sex attraction and equips the body of Christ to address these kinds of issues compassionately without compromising the Word of God.

By Jesus' own definition, a disciple is a person who continues *in His Word* until they are set free by the truth. The church has not emphasized God's Word nearly enough, and it's caused millions of people who claim to be Christians to not live according to what the Bible has to say.

It's not enough just to get saved so you won't go to hell. You have to continue in Jesus' words if you're going to be His disciple. This ought to be the goal of every single Christian! Yet it's amazing how many don't get this. They think the Bible shouldn't influence what they think about economics, racial issues, marriage, or health. When it comes to hot topics like homosexuality, abortion, and evolution, the church is divided and mostly silent.

Some of you reading this may be thinking, *You just need to stick to preaching the Word and stop getting into politics and social issues.* But I am preaching the Word! I'm not the one invading the social and political arenas; these things are encroaching on the church.

Some people argue, "But Jesus said you're just supposed to love one another." They believe that you need to affirm whatever another person believes and accept their behavior, even if it's ungodly. But we need to understand what Jesus actually said after a man came to Him (Matt. 22:36) and asked, *"Master, which is the great commandment in the law?"*

Love Your Neighbor

Jesus said unto him, Thou shalt love the Lord thy God with all thy heart, and with all thy soul, and with all thy mind. This is the first and great commandment. And the second is like unto it, Thou shalt love thy neighbour as thyself. On these two commandments hang all the law and the prophets.

Matthew 22:37–40

Those same people will take what Jesus said—"love your neighbor as yourself"—and say, "You're supposed to be tolerant toward everybody!" They do this to justify ungodly behaviors.

See, if you take the text out of context, all you're left with is a con. If you put what Jesus said back into context, you'll find He was quoting from the Old Testament.

> *Thou shalt not hate thy brother in thine heart: thou shalt in any wise rebuke thy neighbour, and not suffer sin upon him. Thou shalt not avenge, nor bear any grudge against the children of thy people, but thou shalt love thy neighbour as thyself: I am the* LORD.

Leviticus 19:17–18

If you don't rebuke, or warn, a person who you see entering into sin—doing something that is dangerous to them and others—you do not love your neighbor.

I remember one night, when I was driving home, it was very foggy and dark. I live in the mountains of Colorado, and highways curve around rocks where you sometimes can't see what's on the road ahead. On this night, the moon wasn't visible, and you really couldn't see anything.

A man passed me going about fifty-five or sixty miles an hour around a curve, and I saw his brake lights come on. His car jerked to the right, so I slammed on my brakes and came to rest on the shoulder. He was in the right lane, and in the left lane was a horse that he had hit. This horse had caved in his windshield, and the man was slumped over with blood all over him.

As I was trying to help that man, a large SUV came around the corner and hit that horse going fifty miles an hour, launching the vehicle in the air. The driver was able to regain control and stop the car, but she made a dent in the roof where her head hit and was obviously hurt. Then I heard another car coming around the corner! I just had to do something before someone else got hurt.

I ran down the road. It was so dark, you could only see just a few feet ahead. I started jumping out in front of cars that were going fifty and sixty miles an hour, trying to slow them down. People were putting on their brakes and skidding.

I heard horns honk at me. People were yelling stuff— and they weren't telling me just how awesome they thought I was! There's no telling what they thought, and I'm sure there were people offended at me. But when they got around the corner, I bet you some of those same people who cursed me said, "Well, praise God!" They were likely thankful that I had warned them.

Share the Good News

The point is, despite all the honking and yelling, if I hadn't said something to those people, that would've meant I didn't love them. I would have been more concerned about somebody not liking me and being offended than I was about their safety and well-being.

If you don't speak up and tell people the truth, you don't love them. The truth is, you love yourself so much you don't want anybody to roll their eyes at you or say anything negative to you. Instead, we need to stand up for what's right and warn people about the dangers that are ahead if we want to turn this nation around!

I believe we have as much at stake now as we did during the American Revolution when we fought for the independence of this nation. In some ways, I believe it's even more serious now because the attacks are more subtle.

People aren't using guns against us and it's not hand-to-hand combat. It's an ideology that we're fighting.

As much as we need to warn people, we also have to share good reports about what God is doing. We can't just be like those ten spies that went into the Promised Land (Num. 13:33). I was in Washington, DC, several years ago, with David Barton. He occasionally leads tours of the Capitol and Statuary Hall and shares about how many of our founders were clergy and men who loved God.

While we were there, we had a lot of members of Congress come and speak to us, and they were all godly people. I learned they meet together and pray every day. After two days of seeing all these things and hearing these congressional leaders come in and speak, I admitted to David that I had no idea so many good things were happening in this nation. Everything I had been hearing in the news was about how terrible everything is. He responded by saying, "You've been listening to the 'Ten Spies Network.'"

When we were talking about what the Lord showed me about a Third Great Awakening, David told me how he met with a member of Congress about twenty years before. This person had been recently born again and was being discipled on a regular basis. David said this member of Congress told him they believed the nation was already in a Great Awakening based on a number of factors. And that was decades ago!

We need to be sharing about the good things God is doing in this nation and focusing on the positive more than we are the negative. Based on what God has spoken to me and the evidence I've seen that this nation is turning around, I've really been encouraged; and I hope you are too!

Good Things Are Happening

On the morning of August 26, 2019, I was just praising and worshiping God. Over the years, I have recognized a pattern: every twelve years, something really miraculous happens in my life and ministry. At that time, I was at the end of one of these twelve-year periods. So, I asked God, "What's going to happen in the next twelve years?" Immediately, I got the response, "You don't want to know!" I thought to myself that I did want to know, but there was silence after that. God had given me an answer and He wasn't about to argue with me about it.

That was right before the COVID pandemic of 2020, and all the lockdowns and mandates associated with it. The government declared that churches were nonessential and tried to stop people from worshiping. We even received a cease-and-desist letter during one of our events at Charis Bible College. I could have been arrested!

The State of Colorado sued us, and we sued them. Eventually, the U.S. Supreme Court ruled in favor of churches in other states that fought back against lockdowns. Because of that, Colorado backed down and we came through it. Despite all the restrictions we faced in 2020, we set records in nearly every area of our ministry.

For example, our call center took calls remotely, allowing us to keep our Prayer Line open when people needed it the most. Since then, we've been able to grow from just taking calls five days a week during limited hours to seven days a week and twenty-four hours a day. It won't be long before we are taking more than a million phone calls a year. Praise the Lord!

We've increased the number of live streams to our online audience and expanded our television outreach. When we started on television in 2000, our *Gospel Truth* program reached a small percentage of homes in the United States. As of this writing, we have the potential to reach 5.2 billion people around the world just through television, and we are continuing to grow through the Gospel Truth TV network.

Charis has also continued to grow. In 2023, we broke the 1,200-student enrollment barrier at our Woodland Park campus but soon learned that about 600 more students would have come if we just had student housing available. So, I've been sharing with our partners the vision for building a full campus, including housing for individual students and families, a student activities center, more classroom space, a media production building, a conference center and hotel, and more.

We have more than 12,000 Charis graduates around the world who are making an impact and changing lives. Many of them have even gone through our Third-Year Programs—Ministry, Worship, Business, Leadership, Film and Production, Global Training, and Practical Government—and are now influencing culture in a positive way. It's awesome!

"Be Encouraged!"

While I was worshiping and praising God at our Truth & Liberty Conference on September 8, 2023, the Lord put a word on my heart that I believe will really encourage you, and that goes along with all I've been saying in this booklet:

The Lord says that He knows your heart is grieved over things that have happened. His heart is grieved too. But He wants to assure you that, just as He told Elijah there were 7,000 that have not bowed the knee, there are millions in this nation and around the world who have not bowed the knee. And we are in a great move of God. In just a couple of years, you will see it. You will see people who, right now, are shaking their fist in the face of God, they will not even be here. They are going to be removed from positions of leadership. You're going to see things change. And the Lord says to be encouraged. Don't listen to the talk about the giants. Man, greater is He that is with us than he that's with them. So, the Lord says, "You be encouraged!" You are the product of a third great move of God. This conference is a product of the third great move of God. It's already happening. There's a lot to be done. There will be battles. There will be losses. But we win! And God says, "Be encouraged!"[35]

Conclusion

John Adams, the second president of the United States, wrote in 1789, "Our Constitution was designed only for a moral and religious people. It is wholly inadequate for the government of any other."[36] It is not our government that has failed; it's the church that has failed to be the salt of the earth. But I believe things are turning around!

America was founded as a Christian nation. I praise God for the brave men and women who pledged their lives, fortunes, and sacred honor to secure the liberties we have today. They laid the foundation for this nation. I am thankful for the millions who have given their lives in sacrifice to preserve these rights, and I am hopeful that America's best days are still ahead.

I believe we are at a tipping point in the United States. But I also want to encourage you that the Third Great Awakening has already begun, and there is evidence of it everywhere! We are starting to see the fruit of our labor. People are waking up to the truth. We may not have arrived yet at the day when this nation fully embraces godly values—but we've left! And the best is yet to come!

FURTHER STUDY

If you enjoyed this booklet and would like to learn more about some of the things I've shared, I suggest my teachings:

- *God and Country*
- *Christian Philosophy*
- *How to Find, Follow, and Fulfill God's Will*
- *Discover the Keys to Staying Full of God*
- *How to Stay Positive in a Negative World*

These teachings are available either free of charge at **awmi.net** or for purchase in various formats at **awmi.net/store**.

Endnotes

1. "Asbury University Student Uses Map to Track Worshipers Who Came to 'Revival' Services," WDRB-TV, February 24, 2023, https://www.wdrb.com/news/asbury-university-student-uses-map-to-track-worshipers-who-came-to-revival-services/article_a5e03506-b459-11ed-b30e-474a6ca5ff8b.html.

2. Scott Jaschik, "Revival at Asbury Spreads to Other Colleges," Inside Higher Ed, February 19, 2023, https://www.insidehighered.com/quicktakes/2023/02/20/revival-asbury-spreads-other-colleges#:~:text=In%20addition%2C%20the%20revival%20is,Lee%20University%20and%20Cedarville%20University.

3. "Revival Breaks Out at Colleges in Texas and Alabama," Decision Magazine, September 19, 2023, https://decisionmagazine.com/revival-breaks-out-at-colleges-in-texas-and-alabama/.

4. Maria Lencki, "College Students Get Baptized in Pickup Trucks: Jesus Is 'More Powerful' Than Brokenness," Fox News, April 13, 2024, https://www.foxnews.com/media/college-students-baptized-pickup-trucks-jesus-more-powerful-than-brokenness.

5. "A New Chapter in Millennial Church Attendance," Barna Group, August 4, 2022, https://www.barna.com/research/church-attendance-2022/.

6. "The Truth & Liberty Live Call-in Show with Richard Harris & Dr. John Sorenson," Truth & Liberty Show, January 29, 2024, https://truthandliberty.net/episode/the-truth-liberty-live-call-in-show-with-richard-harris-2024-01-29/.

7. "Another Mega Baptism: Church Dunks 1,600+ New Believers on Beach, 'The Spirit of God Is On the Move,'" Talia Wise, CBN News, May 9, 2024, https://www2.cbn.com/news/us/another-mega-baptism-church-dunks-1600-new-believers-beach-spirit-god-move.

8. "Record-Shattering, Massive Baptism in California Compared to 'Book of Acts,'" Charlene Aaron, CBN News, May 23, 2024, https://www2.cbn.com/news/us/record-shattering-massive-baptism-california-compared-book-acts.

9. "The Truth & Liberty Live Call-in Show with Richard Harris & Kelly Shackelford," Truth & Liberty Show, February 6, 2024, https://truthandliberty.net/episode/the-truth-liberty-live-call-in-show-with-richard-harris-2024-02-06/.

10. Kenneth Copeland, "Word Delivered to Andrew Wommack," January 23, 2014, Kenneth Copeland Ministries Ministers' Conference, Eagle Mountain International Church, Newark, TX.

11. William R. Griffith, "The First Great Awakening," American Battlefield Trust. Accessed October 9, 2023, https://www.battlefields.org/learn/articles/first-great-awakening.

12. "Lesson 5: American Republic (Early 1800s–Modern Era)," WallBuilders. Accessed June 26, 2024, https://wallbuilders.com/resource/lesson-5-american-republic-early-1800s-modern-era/.

13. "America's Political Form of Government," *The Founder's Bible* (Newbury Park, CA: Shiloh Road, 2012), 147.

14. "Our Judge, Our Lawgiver, Our King," *The Founder's Bible* (Newbury Park, CA: Shiloh Road, 2012), 1067–68.

15. "The Founding Fathers on Jesus, Christianity and the Bible," WallBuilders, May 29, 2023, https://wallbuilders.com/resource/the-founding-fathers-on-jesus-christianity-and-the-bible/.

16. Tony Perkins, "Nadler on God: He's 'No Concern of This Congress,'" Family Research Council, March 1, 2021, https://www.frc.org/updatearticle/20210301/nadler-god.

17. "The Separation of Church and State," WallBuilders, May 29, 2023, https://wallbuilders.com/resource/the-separation-of-church-and-state/.

18. "Church in the U.S. Capitol," WallBuilders, May 29, 2023, https://wallbuilders.com/resource/church-in-the-u-s-capitol/.

19. "Pro-Life State Policy Maps," Family Research Council, Accessed June 26, 2024, https://www.frc.org/prolifemaps.

20. William Skipworth. "About 32,000 More Babies Being Born Annually in U.S. Since Roe v. Wade Overturned, New Analysis Suggests," Forbes, May 8, 2024, https://www.forbes.com/sites/willskipworth/2023/11/22/about-32000-more-babies-being-born-annually-in-us-since-roe-v-wade-overturned-new-analysis-suggests/?sh=26c6f014f2e1.

21. Tim Pearce, "'Correct The Error': Clarence Thomas Says SCOTUS Should 'Reconsider' Decisions On Contraception, Same-Sex Marriage," *Daily Wire*, June 24, 2022, https://www.dailywire.com/news/correct-the-error-clarence-thomas-says-scotus-should-reconsider-decisions-on-contraception-same-sex-marriage.

22. *Merriam-Webster Dictionary*, s.v. "homosexual." Accessed October 2, 2023, https://www.merriam-webster.com/dictionary/homosexual.

23. William J. Federer, "Who is King in America?," *American Minute*, July 29, 2023, https://americanminute.com/blogs/todays-american-minute/who-is-king-in-america-not-to-vote-is-to-abdicate-the-throne-the-lord-hold-accountable-american-minute-with-bill-federer.

24. Andrew Wommack, "Word from the Lord on the Anniversary of America's Founding," July 4, 2023, Summer Family Bible Conference, Charis Bible College, Woodland Park, CO, https://www.youtube.com/live/AImvVscr6L0?si=89M4-b7tb9EQaVFy&t=2302.

25. Mairead Elordi, "Target Sales Sink After Pride Backlash," *Daily Wire*, August 16, 2023, https://www.dailywire.com/news/target-sales-sink-after-pride-backlash.

26. Lauren Smith, "Disney: A Billion-Dollar Casualty of Woke," Spiked, February 19, 2024, https://www.spiked-online.com/2024/02/19/disney-a-billion-dollar-casualty-of-woke/; Ariel Zilber, "Target Loses $9b in Week Following Boycott Calls Over LGBTQ-Friendly Kids Clothing," New York Post, May 26, 2023, https://nypost.com/2023/05/25/target-loses-8b-in-week-since-boycott-calls-over-pride-collection/; Alyssa Guzman, "Bud Light Sales Still Down 30% Six Months After Dylan Mulvaney Disaster, Drinkers 'Lost Forever': Expert," New York Post, September 9, 2023, https://nypost.com/2023/09/09/bud-light-still-down-30-six-months-after-dylan-mulvaney-partnership/; Taylor Penley, "Planet Fitness Value Plummets $400m After

Transgender Turmoil," Fox Business, March 21, 2024, https://www.foxbusiness.com/media/planet-fitness-value-plummets-transgender-turmoil.

27. Jeff Green and Phil Kuntz, "US Companies Less Vocal on Pride Month During Anti-LGBTQ Outcry," *Bloomberg Law*, June 29, 2023, https://news.bloomberglaw.com/esg/us-companies-less-vocal-on-pride-month-during-anti-lgbtq-outcry.

28. Tim Minella, "Three More States Drop DEI Programs at Their Public Universities," Goldwater Institute, May 14, 2024, https://www.goldwaterinstitute.org/three-more-states-drop-dei-programs-at-their-public-universities/#:~:text=It's%20happening%20at%20the%20University,Diversity%2C%20Equity%2C%20and%20Inclusion.

29. Kiara Alfonseca and Max Zahn, "How Corporate America Is Slashing DEI Workers Amid Backlash to Diversity Programs," ABC News, July 7, 2023, https://abcnews.go.com/US/corporate-america-slashing-dei-workers-amid-backlash-diversity/story?id=100477952.

30. Andrew Wommack, *Christian Philosophy* (Tulsa, OK: Harrison House, 2012), 178.

31. David Barton, "Biblical Literacy," September 9, 2022, Truth & Liberty Coalition Conference, Charis Bible College, Woodland Park, CO, https://www.gospeltruth.tv/watch/?list=63175dbee9b2410001716d5c&id=631bc00dccd4240001f7e429.

32. *Encyclopedia Britannica*, s.v., "The New-England Primer." Accessed October 9, 2023, https://www.britannica.com/topic/The-New-England-Primer.

33. "Pastors Face Communication Challenges in a Divided Culture," Apologetics Workshop, January 29, 2019, https://apologeticsworkshop.wordpress.com/2019/01/29/pastors-face-communication-challenges-in-a-divided-culture/.

34. Charles G. Finney, "The Decay of Conscience," *The [New York] Independent*, December 4, 1873, https://www.gospeltruth.net/1868_75Independent/731204_conscience.htm.

35. Andrew Wommack, "Word from the Lord: Be Encouraged," September 8, 2023, Truth & Liberty Coalition Conference, Charis Bible College, Woodland Park, CO, https://rumble.com/v3g3q8t-truth-and-liberty-coalition-conference-day-2-sessions-7-and-8.html.

36. "From John Adams to Massachusetts Militia, 11 October 1798," Founders Online, National Archives, Accessed June 26, 2024, https://founders.archives.gov/documents/Adams/99-02-02-3102.

Receive Jesus as Your Savior

Choosing to receive Jesus Christ as your Lord and Savior is the most important decision you'll ever make!

God's Word promises, *"That if thou shalt confess with thy mouth the Lord Jesus, and shalt believe in thine heart that God hath raised him from the dead, thou shalt be saved. For with the heart man believeth unto righteousness; and with the mouth confession is made unto salvation"* (Rom. 10:9–10). *"For whosoever shall call upon the name of the Lord shall be saved"* (Rom. 10:13). By His grace, God has already done everything to provide salvation. Your part is simply to believe and receive.

Pray out loud: "Jesus, I acknowledge that I've sinned and need to receive what you did for the forgiveness of my sins. I confess that You are my Lord and Savior. I believe in my heart that God raised You from the dead. By faith in Your Word, I receive salvation now. Thank You for saving me."

The very moment you commit your life to Jesus Christ, the truth of His Word instantly comes to pass in your spirit. Now that you're born again, there's a brand-new you!

Please contact us and let us know that you've prayed to receive Jesus as your Savior. We'd like to send you some free materials to help you on your new journey. Call our Helpline: **719-635-1111** (available 24 hours a day, seven days a week) to speak to a staff member who is here to help you understand and grow in your new relationship with the Lord.

Welcome to your new life!

Receive the Holy Spirit

As His child, your loving heavenly Father wants to give you the supernatural power you need to live a new life. *"For every one that asketh receiveth; and he that seeketh findeth; and to him that knocketh it shall be opened...how much more shall* your *heavenly Father give the Holy Spirit to them that ask him?"* (Luke 11:10–13).

All you have to do is ask, believe, and receive! Pray this: "Father, I recognize my need for Your power to live a new life. Please fill me with Your Holy Spirit. By faith, I receive it right now. Thank You for baptizing me. Holy Spirit, You are welcome in my life."

Some syllables from a language you don't recognize will rise up from your heart to your mouth (1 Cor. 14:14). As you speak them out loud by faith, you're releasing God's power from within and building yourself up in the spirit (1 Cor. 14:4). You can do this whenever and wherever you like.

It doesn't really matter whether you felt anything or not when you prayed to receive the Lord and His Spirit. If you believed in your heart that you received, then God's Word promises you did. *"Therefore I say unto you, What things soever ye desire, when ye pray, believe that ye receive* them, *and ye shall have* them" (Mark 11:24). God always honors His Word—believe it!

We would like to rejoice with you, pray with you, and answer any questions to help you understand more fully what has taken place in your life!

Please contact us to let us know that you've prayed to be filled with the Holy Spirit and to request the book *The New You & the Holy Spirit*. This book will explain in more detail about the benefits of being filled with the Holy Spirit and speaking in tongues. Call our Helpline: **719-635-1111** (available 24 hours a day, seven days a week).

Call for Prayer

If you need prayer for any reason, you can call our Helpline, 24 hours a day, seven days a week at **719-635-1111**. A trained prayer minister will answer your call and pray with you.

Every day, we receive testimonies of healings and other miracles from our Helpline, and we are ministering God's nearly-too-good-to-be-true message of the Gospel to more people than ever. So, I encourage you to call today!

About Andrew Wommack

Andrew Wommack's life was forever changed the moment he encountered the supernatural love of God on March 23, 1968. As a renowned Bible teacher and author, Andrew has made it his mission to change the way the world sees God.

Andrew's vision is to go as far and deep with the Gospel as possible. His message goes far through the *Gospel Truth* television program, which is available to over half the world's population. The message goes deep through discipleship at Charis Bible College, headquartered in Woodland Park, Colorado. Founded in 1994, Charis has campuses across the United States and around the globe.

Andrew also has an extensive library of teaching materials in print, audio, and video. More than 200,000 hours of free teachings can be accessed at **awmi.net**.

About Richard Harris

Richard Harris, executive director of the Truth & Liberty Coalition (founded by Andrew Wommack), is an influential voice in our nation, calling believers to stand for truth in the seven mountains of cultural influence. He co-hosts the weekly Truth & Liberty Live Cast and spearheads Truth & Liberty's work to mobilize believers through media, grassroots activism, and conferences. Richard also founded Richard Harris Ministries, a Christ-centered teaching ministry.

Richard was a successful attorney for twenty-seven years, arguing cases at all levels, including the United States Supreme Court. Richard was instrumental in building the curriculum and plan of study for the Practical Government School at Charis Bible College, a program he also administered for three years. Richard and his wife Donna have three sons.

Contact Information

Andrew Wommack Ministries, Inc.

PO Box 3333
Colorado Springs, CO 80934-3333
info@awmi.net
awmi.net

Helpline: 719-635-1111 (available 24/7)

Charis Bible College

info@charisbiblecollege.org
844-360-9577
CharisBibleCollege.org

For a complete list of all of our offices,
visit **awmi.net/contact-us**.

Connect with us on social media.

 **TRUTH & LIBERTY**

Truth & Liberty is a non-profit based in Woodland Park, Colorado. Established by Andrew Wommack and other Christian leaders, we seek to educate, unify and mobilize believers in Jesus to affect the reformation of nations through the seven mountains of cultural influence.

Our heart is to mobilize the church to engage with biblical truth. Our goal is to educate our audience and connect them with resources and organizations across the nation to help them impact their own spheres of influence.

Truth & Liberty stands for preserving America's constitutional republic of government from the consent of the governed through democratically elected representatives for the purpose of guaranteeing to each citizen their Creator-given rights.

For more information about Truth & Liberty visit
Truthandliberty.net

There's more on the website.

Discover FREE teachings, testimonies, and more by scanning the QR code or visiting awmi.net.

Continue to grow in the Word of God!
You will be blessed!

Your monthly giving makes the greatest kingdom impact

When you give, you make an impact in the kingdom that lasts for generations. Your generosity enables our phone ministers to answer calls 24/7. Your support is also expanding Charis Bible College and allowing *The Gospel Truth* to reach an even wider global audience. You do this and more through your giving each month.

Become a Grace Partner today! Scan the QR code, visit **awmi.net/partne** or call our Helpline at **719-635-1111** and select option five for Partnersh